Uncro

a second selection of my poems

Andy Sutton

Cover conceived and created by Andy Sutton.

Andy Sutton is still a Nottingham based poet who writes poems that rhyme and all that. Mostly.

Social media - The same things are posted to all accounts. There is more of a community on my Facebook page.
- Facebook: facebook.com/andysuttonpoetry
- Instagram: @andysuttonpoetry
- Twitter: @AndySutPoetry

Uncrossed-Out

For Sue – for still being Sue.

Contents

Cinema Food Blues

Crunchy popcorn, crispy treats

Pulled from rustling packets

Remnants of a drink sucked up

Them straws make a racket

Giant buckets filled by scoops

With snacks in that foyer

Each thing that they sell there is an

Audio annoyer

There's no sandwich option or a

Soft snack you could choose

Here in screen sixteen I've got

Those all around me noise abounds these
    eating sounds it seems surround me

Cinema food

B-luuu-ues

Insert Amusing Team Name Here

Huddled round a table
With one appointed scribe
As well as we are able
We answer and imbibe

A singer? No, a film star!
This picture round is hard
Is that Red Rum or Shergar?
Is that Jean-Luc Picard?

The next one is the news round
Events all from this week
We're none of us a news-hound
So "guess" is our technique

The other rounds are taxing
But still we try our best
There's no time for relaxing
As more answers are guessed

It's bar time now, then scoring
We think our chances bleak
Oh no, we're fifth, that's boring
But we'll be back next week

Menace

Have you heard about me?
Heard about my sort?
I want to disturb you
Use you without thought

All for my advantage
Ill begotten schemes
Joy in your discomfort
Punctuates my dreams

Your weakness attracts me
I know it's not right
But I'm not deterred by
Conscience in the night

I know when I hurt you
Pleasure is all mine
Morals do not haunt me
No, I sleep just fine

I Am Not A Robot (The Poem)

This one I think rhymes	This one rhymes most times	This one rhymes quite well	This one's poem hell
I refuse to be defined by robot / non-robot binary paradigms	This one sort of chimes	This one I can't tell	This has rhyming smell
This one falls and climbs	Robots don't like limes	Robot personnel	Robot feels unwell

Not Our Fault

Some residents struggled to get any help when their recently bought flats were deemed unfit for purpose by a report.
www.bbc.co.uk/news/uk-england-london-65668790

Not our fault said insurers
Of that there is no doubt
Exemptions are made very clear
We won't be paying out

Not our fault said the builders
We just followed the spec
We knew it was substandard
What we built was a wreck

Not our fault said designers
They built with dodgy parts
We feel so sad for buyers
It really breaks our hearts

Not our fault said the council
We try to regulate
Residents are all let down
It's such an awful fate

It's someone else's problem
The buyers got a dud
The others need to solve it
We'd all help if we could

Psychic Sammy

My name is Psychic Sammy
I'll tell you what's to be
Your future and your fortune
Just give me 50p

My name is Magic Marty
I'll make you rise and float
And all you need to give me
One crispy five pound note

My name is Doctor Healer
My powers know no bounds
I'll simply lay my hands on you
For just five hundred pounds

My name is Rishi Tory
Just give me all your votes
I'll cure all Britain's problems
By stopping those small boats

That's Torn It

How I learned not to rip up my first drafts.

What I wrote:

I'm leaving you this love letter
On Thursday afternoon
But you told me
That lots of paper rips easily
So I'll scrap this one soon
And sing my love to you instead
All to a loving tune

What they found:

I'm leaving you this
Thursday after
you told me
lots of
crap

Examination Paper 2B – Answer All Questions: What Is Education For?

To learn? To take in? To know?
To absorb and retain facts?
To train? To instruct? To grow?
To change the ways we act?

To teach us how to sit in rows
And do as we are told?
To make people more useful
Until they are too old?

To maintain the
Elitist structure?
To subvert the
Elitist structure?

To just be a commodity
Student customers can buy?
To make worker commodities
For industries to hire?

To compare competing students
Then test them and select?
To get enquiring students to
Ask questions and reflect?

To make all our lives better?
To free up constrained thoughts?
To help understand others?
To enable curious sorts?

To aid tolerance and cooperation?
To enrich lives? To inspire?
To give joy? To lift our spirits?
To help us all reach higher?

Discuss.

Part

Part is a character's role in a play

Part is when visitors go on their way

Part's a component replaced when gone wrong

Part is an instrument's piece in your song

Part is a broadcast which others preceded

Part is a spare one that's stored until needed

Part is what hair does (unless you have none)

Part is what's left when a portion has gone

Parts are essential if wholes are to be

Part is what you are of me

If Facebook Algorithms Applied To The Rest Of Life

One fine Monday morning I woke up
Had tea and some cornflakes to eat
Went upstairs to wake up my children
With their favoured sweet breakfast treat
The kids were nowhere to be seen though
Those algo things they got me beat

Next thing I began my commuting
I need to get my hard-earned pay
But at the bus stop I kept waiting
Not one bus was coming my way
My boss tells me now I'm reported
Those algo things they spoil my day

When I got home later that evening
My sister banged hard on my door
Insisting she rang me and rang me
It's too many calls to ignore
My phone's showing no missed calls from her
Those algo things struck me once more

As normal I went out to Tesco
It's time for my grocery shop
They've got no bread, butter, or biscuits
No veg, no red wine, and no pop
So I went home laden with mad stuff
Those algo things they've got to stop!

How She Replied

That very first time

He said what he thought

He'd thought it before

This time it was caught

In faltering voice

From somewhere inside

Three words that 'til now

By instinct he'd hide

And now they were out

No longer denied

And all was now hung

On how she replied

That moment of wait

So hard to get through

'Til she said her part

"And I love you too"

Zips

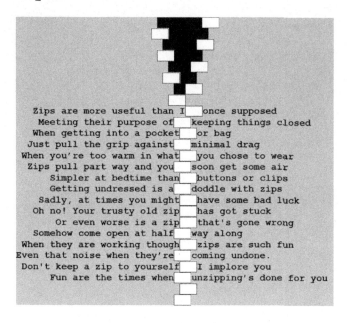

Zips are more useful than I once supposed
Meeting their purpose of keeping things closed
When getting into a pocket or bag
Just pull the grip against minimal drag
When you're too warm in what you chose to wear
Zips pull part way and you soon get some air
Simpler at bedtime than buttons or clips
Getting undressed is a doddle with zips
Sadly, at times you might have some bad luck
Oh no! Your trusty old zip has got stuck
Or even worse is a zip that's gone wrong
Somehow come open at half way along
When they are working though zips are such fun
Even that noise when they're coming undone.
Don't keep a zip to yourself I implore you
Fun are the times when unzipping's done for you

Winter's Tale

Got up after much delay

Cold air's savage greeting

Porridge keeps the chill at bay

That relief is fleeting

Staying home is not okay

Body warmth depleting

Household bills too high to pay

Shopping bills competing

Go to somewhere warm I say

Comfortable seating

Maybe to that great café

Surely that's not cheating

All to just get through today, and

Not switch on my heating

A Poet's Morning

It's just ten percent inspiration

Keep working your poem they say

I'd left open my bedroom window

And felt the first draught of the day

I can't write my verses while sober

So second draught was I.P.A.

And now that I've written some words here

My third draft is well underway

Dads' Race

Primary school sports day
My kids thought me fitter
In that way that kids do
Thought me a big hitter

"Dad" they urged "Will you run?
Please don't let us down!
We think you're the fastest!
Claim that dads' race crown!"

Well into my forties
On the starting line
I'm an older father
And drink too much wine

In fear I looked sideways
Each of them looked fast
All looked in their twenties
Phew! I wasn't last!

A Grammar Pedant's Romance

When you're far away from me

Life seems so unfair

I'm unsettled as can be

Like a misspelled "there"

When you're home and hugging me

I feel like I'm from a

Special place I'm meant to be

Like an Oxford comma

Say Goodbye To The Circus

Ignore all you know about Dumbo

Nellie has nothing to say

Trunks may be cute but forget them

They're not important today

Once they were noble and needed

We thought them quite elegant

But things change and now the grey beasts are

Totally irrelephant

Some Words

Some words are heavy and some words are light
Some words are dim while yet others are bright
Some words are **thick** and of course some are thin
Some are quite blunt and some sharp like a pin
Some words are rainbows while some are just plain
Some get said over again and again and again
Some will not straighten they just like to bend
Some are not happy unless at the *end*

Three Things

Got home at roughly six-thirty

Three things to do on my mind

First was to get out of work clothes

Second was open some wine

Third was world peace for all people

Wrote down those three things to do

Here's why I feel optimistic:

By seven I'd done the first two

Shame

I see timid ten-year-old me
Meeting mates
A confident if unthreatening gang
On the constant walk to school
He didn't quite know
That in the jumper knitted by his mum
Was a capable boy
Thought pleasant and well behaved

Later in his school blazer
The playground now the school yard
He was neither
By instinct nor intent
A racist, homophobe, or misogynist
But to fit in
He left unchallenged
And sometimes echoed
The cruel words of his mates
Who surely also
Neither meant nor understood them
After all only similar boys occupied
His too small world
In that learning place where he learned
Little of his later world

And though now ashamed
Still timid and
In confident if unthreatening gangs
I'm finally me

Auto Unknowns

When I push a trolley round Tesco

Tossing in things I like best

The price that all those things add up to

Is roughly the total I guessed

When I'm buying tickets for concerts

A local act or major star

It always costs more than I hoped but

My guess is not normally far

When I take my car to be serviced

And further repairs must be made

I don't know will it be, say, fifty

Or five hundred pounds to be paid

Uncrossed-Out

A tea mug that sits undisturbed on the shelf

The music I don't want to hear by myself

You are what I notice when you are not here

Your absence made tangible while you're not near

You're my bathroom's mystery bottles and jars

The passenger seat next to mine in my car

You're food in my fridge that I rarely would choose

A crossword with untackled, uncrossed-out clues

You're unwatched recordings of Only Connect

You're my dog's excuse to feign lonely neglect

You are what I notice when you are not near

These things I don't want when I wish you were here

Things You Can Say About Poetry Or Sex

A short one is just fine but it's good to take your time

Manuals can help but to wing it is sublime

Some say turn the lights down but others disagree

"Show don't tell" is helpful when you do it properly

Rhythm is important so keep a steady beat

Sedentary is boring you should try it on your feet

Learn the rules then break them for maximum effect

Many people find out that oral helps connect

Adjectives are handy but they can be overdone

Never, ever fake it or you may spoil all the fun

Pedant's Lament

My love wondered why she's blocked
Like I never knew her
Turned out that she would not say
"Eight items or fewer"

And she would use upper case
Writing breeds like "beagles"
Then would add a quite wrong "The"
Naming the band "Eagles"

But I'm sad and lonely now
My love life in tatters
Causing me to wonder if
All this really matters

So My Dear come back to me
Please accept this token
I'll forgive you said your heart
Literally was broken

Collector Who

(Dedicated to my friend Dave)

You can never have too many daleks

According to one of my friends

I think that he's planning a show down

A time when humanity ends

He's hundreds all stored in his bedroom

They're plastic and some are quite small

But if he's got large enough numbers

That won't be a problem at all

He's training them all I imagine

To change our society's fate

With one simple goal in their mindset

Exterminate! Exterminate!

Black Friday

(This is about the absurdity of Black Friday sales in the UK)

Thanksgiving gives two days of leisure
For all of us in the UK
Big part of our cultural story
We celebrate this special day

Fourth Thursday that falls in November
A great UK bank holiday
And Friday no work for us either
"So let's all go shopping" we say

All UK stores think this is lovely
A day when so many will shop
"Let's have a big sale on that Friday
Our till ringing surely won't stop"

To stimulate trade before Christmas
All British shops think it's the best
And all because we love Thanksgiving
Bank hols, pumpkin pie, and the rest

We're wise shoppers not fooled by nonsense
For which I think we should be glad
Without our bank hols for Thanksgiving
Black Friday UK would be mad

Only Love

Saying "He said he loved her"

Where could an "only" go

Only he said he loved her

No-one else told her so

He only said he loved her

He didn't mean it though

He said only he loved her

No rival from a foe

He said he only loved her

From there might friendship grow

He said he loved only her

What she desired to know

Comfort

There's plenty more fish in the sea, son
Said mum to her troubled lad Jack
But he didn't care about sea life
He just wanted Grace to call back

You're still only young, she continued
You're handsome and clever as well
You'll break hearts and have your heart broken
So move on, regroup, and don't dwell

And really you could do much better
She's not good enough for my boy
She made you do all of the running
Her voice, well it used to annoy

Mum had just tried to be helpful
Her son had more pleasures in store
But when you're fifteen it's no comfort
Her words they just made him hurt more

Brackets

Brackets are useful (they keep up a shelf)

Brackets are easy (you fit them yourself)

Brackets are metal (OK, some are wood)

Brackets are sturdy (if they're any good)

Brackets are cheap (ish) (though stout ones are dearer)

Brackets have words in (to make the point clearer)

A Lesson

(This is completely true)

I once helped teach English
To some refugees
Helping them learn phrases
So their stay might ease

Once we covered 'thanking'
"Cheers", "Thankyou", and "Thanks"
And where you might say these
Shops, cafés, and banks

Acting situations
Where thanks are expressed
They asked me "Of all these
Which one is the best?"

These poor souls I knew must
Cope with daily shite
But their main concern was
How to be polite

Fading Scribbles

Kids you grew up faster

Than scribbles fade away

Drawings on the fridge door

Those are here to stay

I miss noisy antics

Messy, crazy play

Splashy, frothy bath times

Toys left in the way

Loved helping with homework

But honestly I say

I love even more the

Grown-ups you are today

Litterally

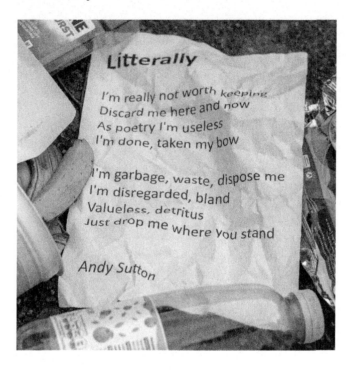

Litterally

I'm really not worth keeping
Discard me here and now
As poetry I'm useless
I'm done, taken my bow

I'm garbage, waste, dispose me
I'm disregarded, bland
Valueless, detritus
Just drop me where you stand

Andy Sutton

Lines

Children have crayons for things that are duller
Lines are the things not to cross when they colour
If there's a coupon or offer you spotted
Lines are a guide for your scissors (when dotted)
So they can say the right things at their turn
Lines are the words that an actor must learn
If you are naughty or acting the fool
Lines are a punishment when you're at school
Working conditions are not as they'd like
Lines are for pickets emboldened by strike
In the UK this is not what we say
Lines are our queues in the U.S. of A.
Diagram makers need visual guides
Lines are connectors or area sides
Maths has some concepts that one must embrace
Lines are to show one-dimensional space
Travelling smoothly, best not to be late
Lines are for trains taking people or freight
Poetry writers like making points clear
Lines are in verses like this last one here

After Work

Being tired is the norm

When you're working age

Lots of time is spent each week

Just to earn your wage

So at this time of my life

Pension pays the bills

I thought I'd be full of life

Without those work ills

But exhaustion strikes again

Work cannot be blamed

So I find that I'm re-tired

And that's how it got named

Poetic Licence

Often but not all the time
Things I write will be in rhyme
Much as I don't like to lie
Poet's licence gets me by
If the meaning's not absurd
I rhyme an untruthful word

I just can't see where the hurt is
If I claim I'm in my thirties
Or I'll stretch the truth a bit
Since in rhyme I'm super fit
And though not exactly true
I'll tell you I'm six foot two

Ask my job and I'll reply
I'm an international spy
"Who's my friend?" you might demand
I'll tell you it's Russell Brand
Education pass or fail?
I did rather well at Yale

My clothes should you wish to know
All are sourced from Savile Row
What car do I drive by choice?
Hand-built luxury Rolls Royce
Finest wine to grace my table?
I get Aldi's cheap own label

Facebook Posts To Ignore

Post from ill-informed debater

"Look for our announcement later"

Jokey challenge then "I'll start"

"If you solve this you are smart"

"X percent will not repost"

Pictures of a Sunday roast

"It was better way back when"

"Here's me at a gig, again"

Classroom Walls

(Written after reading news reports about schools closing because of crumbling concrete)

Through my school days I would fumble

Some subjects I'd stall and mumble

During games I'd fail and stumble

Much of it has made me humble

Classroom walls displayed our jumble

Never did I think they'd crumble

Proof Of Age

The man who delivered my parcel

Saught proof that I'm over eighteen

My passport's upstairs in a folder

Should I run up? I wasn't keen

He peered in the room from my doorway

Taking in things he could see

My slippers, my statins, my vinyl

The photos of children and me

My record deck with its big speakers

My senior railcard as well

I asked "Should I go fetch my passport?"

He said "No, you're old, I can tell"

Gloating Ode To Being Retired

Every day's a jeans day

Calm, and routine free

Hobbies after breakfast

Then all day 'til tea

Outside when there's sunshine

Inside when there's not

Meeting friends and talking

Reading quite a lot

Snoozing if I want to

Poems when inspired

Photos while out walking

All 'cause I'm retired

Reasons To Stay For Just One More

...

The landlord looks sad so I'll help if I'm able

The dog's asleep peacefully under the table

I do love this music they're playing today

I've heard that good beer keeps a sore throat at bay

It's Jane's twenty first and we need to mark that

It's sunny outside and I've not got my hat

It's cloudy outside and there might be a shower

I just missed my bus and they come every hour

They've got this guest beer which is lovely to drink

It's National Glass Day, or something, I think

Norse Code

(At the time of writing this there was a craze for posting Facebook photos of oneself transformed to look like a Viking)

Who wants to know

How I'd look when I'm biking?

Why would that pic

Be to anyone's liking?

Maybe a photo of me

While I'm hiking?

Or while I'm drunk

When the alcohol's spiking?

After a makeover

That would be striking

But nowadays seems

We're all going Viking

(And They Called It) Poppy Love

"Love is like oxygen"

The Sweet sang in their day

"Love is the drug" we all

Heard Roxy Music say

"Love bites" (and also bleeds)

Def Leppard chose to sing

I learned from old pop music

That love's a mixed-up thing

Top Marks

Let's give all A pluses

Firsts for all degrees

Great that we encourage

Wonderful to please

Each of them deserves it

All of them the best

Don't pass just the good ones

Top marks for the rest

Do this too with driving

All learners prevail

Some though causing mayhem

Can't be labelled "fail"

When it comes to doctors

It's not what they know

Pick those who at uni

Had a decent go

Reader Feedback

Could you reflect
Then please select
The answers that apply

- o I like the style
- o It's quite worthwhile
- o I found it worth a try
- o I think it's good
- o He wrote a dud
- o I hate it, I won't lie
- o I like this verse
- o No, now it's worse

Now in this box say why

Trawlers

I'm trawling social media

I'm searching on TV

For things I can complain of

As though they've upset me

I'm parsing every sentence

I'm reading every word

It might be what I watched or

What I read or heard

It doesn't have to hurt me

It may not quite offend

With some imagination

It's easy to pretend

Celebs had best be careful

Not just those who've done wrong

We'll try then find all guilty

My online, righteous throng

Fitted Sheet

You're more helpful than I can measure

Like a fitted sheet

You're neat which gives a certain pleasure

Like a fitted sheet

I hope you know you're much desired

Like a fitted sheet

Ironing you would make me tired

(I don't iron you

But if I did

You'd be)

Like a fitted sheet

(I also don't iron fitted sheets

So actually

You are like a fitted sheet after all)

Audiofile

Don't need psychometrics
No test analyses
Diagnose your friends by
How they store LPs

Alphabet's important
By artist I suggest
Then within the artist
Release date is the best

Band or person surname
"The" or "A" ignored
Check there is a logic
How their music's stored

If there is no order
Or discs not put back
Terminate the friendship
Ditch that maniac

Loxley Loyalty

"Let's rethink, tonight, at the forest"
Cried Robin, who travelled on foot
With Merry Men ever beside him
For in him their faith they had put

From Nottingham Castle they journeyed
At four hours they're maybe halfway
They'd barely make Sherwood by sunset
Long walk, twenty miles in one day

"We'll head back again in the morning!
We'll yet make that sheriff atone!"
The Merry Men, weary from walking
Cried "No Rob, you go on your own"

Indie Cinema

A film just came out that looks worthy
I guess I'll book tickets and see
It's showing this week so on Thursday
I'll pick up Yvonne if she's free

You know we forgo multiplexes
We feel indie cinema's best
Don't care if the seats aren't so comfy
We're there to improve not to rest

And sure the sound isn't so hi fi
But look what it offers instead
A café where people sit loudly
Discussing the books that they've read

It's vital we look a bit arty
Then tell one and all that we've been
It's not that we go there to see things
We go there, of course, to be seen

Passwordpassword$1

"You must reset your password"

I'm told on my device

"Your password must be longer"

I type the same word twice

"Can't be the same as last time"

I swap to something new

"It must contain a symbol"

A dollar sign will do

"It must contain a number"

So 'one' goes in last place

"At least one capital please"

So start with upper case

At last it's let me change it!

The feeling's quite sublime

But there's no way that I will

Type it in right next time

Don't Be Bored

"I am bored my dear" he said

"Sneak on board, don't fear" she pled

Next they slip their daughter in

But the ship let water in

"Thought the boat was wood" said he

"Tasked to float, it should" said she

Boat skipper explained "It would

This ship's well maintained, that's good

Hull is board, and firm, that's great

But was bored by worm of late"

Is It Just Me?

Self-help posts annoy me
When I go online
Pointing out I'm faultless
Innocent, and fine

Telling me I'm worthy
Always good and fair
No-one criticise me
Critics! Head elsewhere!

I should tell the doubters
Get out of my brain
You've no right to be there
I don't need that pain

Thing about these posts is
Since they're everywhere
All of us receive them
Fail of logic there

Really it's all nonsense
Let's have this no more
I'm at least as flawed as
Those I should ignore

Did The Earth Move?

I'd just done my grocery shopping online
A survey popped up straight away
They wondered if I'd spare a bit of my time
To say how I'd liked it today
Yes Asda, the shopping went perfectly well
I'll give you a maximum score
I easily browsed all the things that you sell
An easy to navigate store

Your virtual helper did all that they could
A competent job I would say
They easily earned a full five ("Very Good")
They even wished me a good day
I found all the items I wanted this week
Would I recommend you? Well, yes
No, can't think of anything more I would seek
To yield better shopping success

So now, like last week, I'll press "Send" on my phone
And give you my ten out of ten
This order's been as good as any I've known
Then Thursday I'll do it again
I hope that this next bit won't hurt you too much
My loyalties can fall elsewhere
I've surveys from others who've now been in touch
For they also want me to care

I booked for the cinema I must reveal
Reserved a room in an old inn
The council have asked me to say how I feel
Since mailing re unemptied bin
It takes quite a chunk out of my time each day
The surveys today total nine
Relentless these feedback forms coming my way
If ever I do things online

Pitter Patter

In summer nineteen-sixty-nine
We'd booked a holiday
Us kids, we were excited
We're gonna go away

A holiday park beckoned
With static caravans
Seaside resort on Yorkshire's coast
I made so many plans

On Saturday arrived on site
Moved in for one week's stay
Unpack our things, explore around
There's lots of scope to play

Day one we planned to hit the beach
Just down the local lane
But played cards in the caravan
With sounds of falling rain

Day two we planned to hit the slots
Amusements on my brain
Yet played cards in the caravan
With sounds of falling rain

Day three I asked for crazy golf
My sisters don't complain
But more cards in the caravan
With sounds of falling rain

Day four a seal trip's on the cards
But that hope seems in vain
We played cards in the caravan
With sounds of falling rain

Day five I've rather given up
No point in plans again
It's more cards in the caravan
With sounds of falling rain

Remaining days are all alike
We no longer complain
We like cards in the caravan
With sounds of falling rain

Decluttering

I tried to declutter my house once

It seemed like a good thing to do

I got rid of books and old clothing

Odd tools and some ornaments too

I worry I went a bit further

Than I _ _ _ intended to go

I got _ _ _ of _ _ _ _ _ that are useful

It _ _ _ a _ _ _ silly I _ _ _ _

Feelings Reign

Slowly he got on the train

Someone she'd not meet again

Out she walked into the rain

Where her wrath could start to wain

Thoughts of him still in her brain

Some of fun, but most of pain

Though she'd never quite explain

Part of him still would remain

Shakespeare's Jokes

When people laugh at Shakespeare

Whose jokes are fairly rare

It's not because they're funny

It's 'cause they know they're there

Phew

(Apposite for any late summer or autumnal heatwave)

Summer sun's been not a lot

July, August this not

This month shows what it's still got

Crikey, blimey, phew, it's hot

Changing The Clocks

One season an hour is added

The other one's taken away

Spring forward or spring back or something

Or is it fall backwards we say?

My tip to relieve this confusion

And, frankly, to always sleep more

Is move them back both spring and autumn

Always gain an hour to snore

Palinimerick

The limerick lines won't seem smart

If they're in reverse

It might seem perverse

A couplet keeps some lines apart

It's normal for two rhymes to start

It's normal for two rhymes to start

A couplet keeps some lines apart

It might seem perverse

If they're in reverse

The limerick lines won't seem smart

Joined Up

At school, tongue on upper lip
Learned the shape of "a"
"b" and "c" and all the rest
Practiced every day

Later joined them into words
Sat just on the line
"Neater, neater!" teacher said
Words then could combine

Cursive writing, all joined up
Punctuation next
Pencils were replaced with pens
Copy from the text

Thus I learned to write my words
All looked as they should
What I learned to write about
Sadly not so good

Work was teaching of a world
Crime and lives impure
Which neat writing never could
Define, explain, or cure

Battle Of The Bands

"I win" said the elastic

"For I can stretch and hold"

"No way" cried some musicians

"We're entertainment gold"

Then NHS employees

Said "We are many grades"

"But we can keep your hair straight

The hairband never fades"

The judges had no option

For all were rightly proud

They said "To stop the fighting

You're banned, you're not allowed"

When The Bard Breaks

When Shakespeare's away overnight

He likes a place airy and light

Quite near a pub

With good morning grub

These things will entice him to write:

"To Airbnb or not to Airbnb, that is the question."

If Sofia Coppola Had Written A Poem Instead

"Perdido" if you're in Brazil
In Spanish it's "perdido" still
Finland folk say "eksynit"
"Verloren" Germans say for it
"Perdu" if by any chance
You stray from the map in France
"Verdwaald" may help very much
Seeking pointers from the Dutch
"Perso" could aid getting home
If you went off-course in Rome
"Försvunnen"'s the word to Swedes
"Tabt" in Danish might yield leads
"Kayip" a useful Turkish word
"Bortkommen" in Norway, I've heard
"Zagubiony" for the Poles
"Izgubljen" for Croatian souls

"bị lạc đường" if you have strayed
Should get Vietnamese aid
Prague can be a tricky trek
"Ztracený" should work in Czech
Now when in another nation
You will know "Lost in Translation"

Songs

I like a song that's beaty
I like a song that's blue
I like a song with words that
Hit my soul right through

I like a song that's clever
Or gets stuck in my ear
I like to hear an oldie
Or one released this year

I like a song that's raw or
A song skilfully played
But when you've really got me
Please don't repeat and fade
Please don't repeat and fade
Please don't repeat and fade
Please don't repeat and fade

A Day Off Work

There's a rookie error
People often make
Not seeking most pleasure
That is their mistake

If you are a worker
For five days a week
With alarms to wake you
It's to you I speak

When you go to bed and
Next day you're on leave
Or bank hols like May Day
Do not be naïve

Please keep your alarm set
It will sound at seven
When it rings just turn it off
Stay in bed! That's heaven!

Anyone For ...?

Underarm, overarm, volleying free

The watchers of Wimbledon tennis are we

Hoping the sun and the clouds will be kind

And British players won't get left behind

Henman, Raducanu, we can remember the games

When the ball landed on the lines

With their towels unfurled

Serving with racquets to take them to six games to love

Microsoft's Trip To Mars

A spaceship went to Mars one day
With all the latest tech
Whether it all worked or not
Someone forgot to check

The outer hatch was asking for
A password from the crew
Letters, numbers, symbols that
It seems none of them knew

Their helmets were not ever used
A snag they could not fix
Since helmet version 4.5
Won't fit suit 4.6

The ship's software was fine on Earth
With friendly interface
But T&Cs that no-one read
Don't license it for space

So this tech firm's trip into space
Ended with no survivor
Since the rocket home failed too
Without the latest driver

A Brief Encounter With Sir John

I bumped into Betjeman, really!

On Sunday, near noon I would say

I'd got off a train at St Pancras

And there he was stood, plain as day

It wasn't a moving encounter

I'd hoped for connection with me

The problem with poets in stations

They tend to be stationary

My Qualifications

Round about age four I earned
"Certificate of Cheek"
A "Permit for Self-Serving"
I think came that same week

Age eleven sat and passed
A "Mock and Sneer Exam"
Ignored teachers and became
The thinker that I am

Sat a few GCSEs
Passed well in "Ranting Studies"
Grade 'A' "Spouting After Beer"
(Practiced with my buddies)

I've A-levels in "Talking Rot"
And "Lying Skills (Applied)"
Did quite well in "Bluffing Through"
Took "Moaning" in my stride

Uni beckoned so I read
"BA Undermining"
Passed with honours, then I got
A PhD in "Whining"

Now in Facebook post debates
People can't decide
I wade in and put them right
'Cause I am qualified

Nation States

Land of paying lenders

That's a Divination

Country of spoon benders

That's a Urination

Where they're blocking rivers

Call it a Damnation

Male deer give you shivers

When you're in Stagnation

Parrots have a ball

When in Pollination

Vehicles free to all

Welcome to Carnation

Driving door to door

Land of Incarnation

Pause driving then more

Ah! Reincarnation

Nominative Deliberations

If young Nathan sleeps for months

Does he hiber*Nate?*

If Queen Kathryn quits the throne

Does she abdi*Kate?*

Lawrence uses lots of words

That's vocabu*Larry*

Caroline makes potions in

An old apothe*Carrie*

Days

The strong start is on Monday

I don't mean in a fun way

It then goes downhill I say

The weak end comes on Friday

She Is Not Alone

Janet has a good job

Ethical and just

Looking after creatures

Is for her a must

In the world of garments

Mammal skins are used

And when Janet sees them

She is not amused

So she checks on outlets

Welfare on her mind

Hoping she does not have

Clothes encounters of the furred kind

Fame

She wanted it so much that

One day when it came near

With folded arms and breath held

She made it disappear

Tory Helpline

Hi, welcome to our helpline
Conservative HQ
Now please select an option
So we can best help you
Press one if you're donating
So you become a lord
Press two for raising rent to
What most cannot afford
Press three if you are rich but
You want to pay less tax
Press four if you're campaigning
And need to hide some facts
Press five if you're a racist
To keep out foreign sorts
Press six to stop all victims
Arriving at our ports
Press seven if all laws are
For commoners, not you
Press eight to shrink our healthcare
So hospitals are few
Press nine to hide your finance
And keep your funds offshore
Press hash to vote us out if
You can't take any more

The Poet Of Christmas Past

Did you spy the door knocker changing?
Did your ears hear chains being hauled?
Which foretell three poets shall join you
Past, Present, Future we're called

It's too late to hope you'll escape us
The dice of this haunting is cast
The first one is nigh, so be ready
The Poet of Christmases Past

Some two-thousand times have I been here
Plus twenty-three more years are gone
It's hard to remember at my age
They sort of all merge into one

Christmas began in year zero
Long before reindeer and sprouts
Long before Dudley Moore elf had
Some awkward but logical doubts

First one was small, in a stable
Though much of it seems like a blur
Was it gold that was left as a gift then?
But frankincense, really? And myrrh?

Along came performing of pantos
With low rent celebrity cast
I tell you, be glad each one's over
Those terrible Christmases past

Forgettable X Factor singles
Except Rage Against the Machine
And tiresome John Lewis adverts
We've even had Covid nineteen

When young they were full of excitement
With so many markets and fairs
I'm too old for that, I'm just grateful
If I know why I came upstairs

So watch out for someone much sharper
Who champions worker and peasant
And offers more cynical views as
The Poet of Christmas that's Present

The Poet Of Christmas Present

I am the second poet, hark
For I was born this year
This present Christmas day will mark
My only one I fear

This my poem's bland I know
No wisdom, love, nor fun
This festive verse is bland ho, ho
And random rhyming's done

These solstice words are cheery chose
But merry sense it's not
In rhyme that snowman's carrot nose
A manger child begot

A human would not write this worse
It's like I did not try
For this the present Christmas verse
Is written by A.I.

The Poet Of Christmas Future

It's Christmas twenty-thirty-four
We can't afford the heating
Simon Cowell, prime minister
Just gave his TV greeting

We can't play Slade, or Elton John
No Chris de Burgh, nor Bing
They all got cancelled by the throng
No classics left to sing

No gifts to buy in decked out shops
We order gifts online
You can't use precious paper wrap
Or you may get a fine

But still we meet at grandma's home
We eat, we hug, we joke
And uncle tells his raucous tales
When he's had rum and coke

The kids are well excited too
'Cause Santa's on his way
And there's "The Snowman" on TV
It's great is Christmas Day

Homing In On Santa

We think your words amusing
No single phrase that bores
So at your show at Christmas
There's more than Scant Applause

I've talons sharp and piercing
Not fingernails like yours
They're orange-brown at Christmas
For I have Sandy Claws

I lurk inside a contract
I clarify your laws
Four legal lines at Christmas
For I'm a Stanza Clause

I'm tired of all this wordplay
My name has no such flaws
I bring you gifts at Christmas
For I am Santa Clause

Resolutions

New Year's Resolutions
For twenty-twenty-four
Won't be the same as last year
They failed so I need more

Last time they were restrictive
Enjoyment has been less
Eat none of this, cut back on that
Try harder to progress

So this time they'll be selfish
Resolve to have good times
See friends and go to concerts
Take photos and write rhymes

Make time to smile, relax, and dance
Wear clothes that suit my mood
Late bed times, play more games, and
Enjoy well-chosen food

Printed in Great Britain
by Amazon